piano / vocal / guitar

kirk franklin hero

ISBN 1-4234-0874-8

HAL•LEONARD®
CORPORATION
7777 W. BLUEMOUND RD. P.O. BOX 13819 MILWAUKEE, WI 53213

Visit Hal Leonard Online at
www.halleonard.com

contents

LOOKING FOR YOU

Words and Music by KIRK FRANKLIN,
SHEREE BROWN, CHARLES MIMS,
PATRICE RUSHEN and FRED WASHINGTON

Moderately fast Disco

(Spoken:)
To all my people in the struggle, you think God's forgotten about you. Here's some pain medicine.

You're in your car,

you're at the house, *on your job,* *be encouraged, boo.*

HERO

Words and Music by
KIRK FRANKLIN

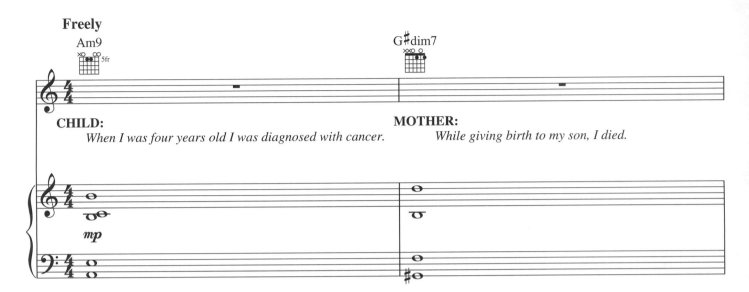

CHILD: *When I was four years old I was diagnosed with cancer.*

MOTHER: *While giving birth to my son, I died.*

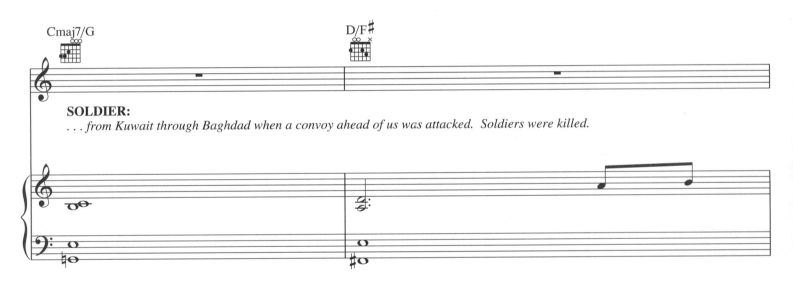

SOLDIER: *. . . from Kuwait through Baghdad when a convoy ahead of us was attacked. Soldiers were killed.*

MOTHER: *I lost nearly ninety percent of the blood in my body.*
They had to amputate my

CHILD: *The doctor didn't know if I was going to live.*

Vocals written one octave higher than sung.

LET IT GO

Words and Music by
KIRK FRANKLIN

Rap I: *(See rap lyrics)*
Rap II: *(See rap lyrics)*
Rap III: *(See rap lyrics)*

With pedal throughout

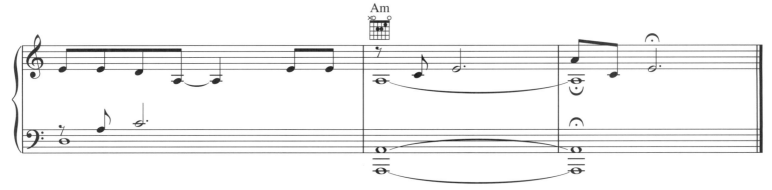

Rap Lyrics

Rap I:

My momma gave me up when I was four years old.
She didn't destroy my body but she killed my soul.
Now it's cold, 'cause I'm sleeping in my back seat.
I understand the spirit's willing, but my flesh is weak.
(Let him speak.) Let me speak.
I never had a chance to dream.
Ten years old and finding love in dirty magazines.
Ms. December, you remember I bought you twice.
Now I'm thirty plus and still paying the price.

Had a sister that I barely knew.
Kind of got separated by the age of two.
Same momma, different daddy, so we couldn't fake it.
I saw my sister's daddy beat her in the tub, naked.
Take it serious, the demons in a man's mind.
The same man on rape charges; now he's doing time.
Crack followed, and like daddy, prison, thirteen years.
Haven't seen her. I guess she's traded tears for fears.

Rap II:

Sex was how I made it through.
Without someone to teach you love, what else was there to do?
See, where I'm from they call you gay,
Say you ain't a man. Show 'em you ain't no punk.
Get all the girls you can: a simple plan that
    still haunts me even now, today.
Back to seventeen and got a baby on the way.
No GED. All I see is failure in my eyes.
If you're listening and remember, I apologize.

I was raised failing in the church.
Made mistakes and heard the Lord's calling in the church.
At the service, in the parking lot, getting high.
Wanted to be accepted so bad, I was willing to die.
Even tried to tell the pastor, but he couldn't see years
    of low self esteem and insecurities.
Church taught me how to shout and how to speak in tongues,
But preacher, teach me how to live now when the tongue is done.

Rap III:

Jesus, please, on my knees, can't You hear my crying?
You said to put it in Your hands,
    and Lord, I'm really trying.
You wasn't lying when You said
    you reap what you sow.
Like that night momma died, it's hard to let it go.
You adopted me, cared for me, changed my name
But I cursed at you, lied to you and left you pain.
It's not strange; I can still see it in my head
To know for hours you were lying there in that bed.

If you're listening to this record, if it's day or night,
If your momma is still living, treat your momma right.
Don't be like me and let that moment slip away.
And be careful, 'cause you can't take back what you say.
To my real momma, if you're listening, I'm letting it go.
To my father, I forgive you, 'cause you didn't know
    that the pain was the preparation for my destiny.
And one more thing, Lord, let my son be a
    better man than me.

Ad lib.:

Shout.
I'm trying to let it go; can't You hear me?
I'm talking to you, you in the corner,
    you in the back. Come on.

You don't have to take your life.
You don't have to cut your wrists.
You don't have to hide behind sex. Come on.

IMAGINE ME

Words and Music by
KIRK FRANKLIN

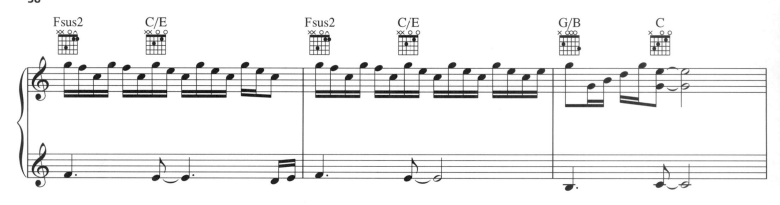

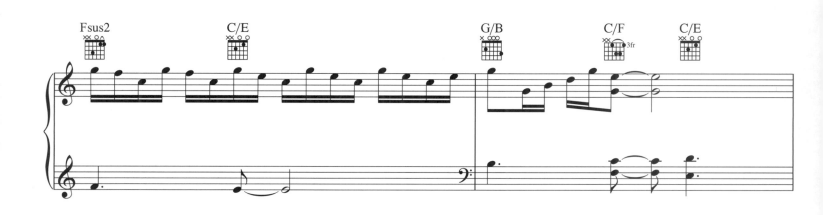

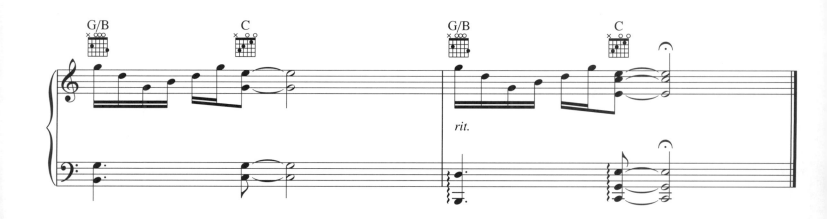

COULD'VE BEEN

Words and Music by
KIRK FRANKLIN

You e - nough. No mat - ter how hard I try, ____ Je - sus,

I re - al - ize ____ it could've been tears in my eyes cry - ing, See, it's
("Lord, ‿ please get me

eas - y to com - plain when you don't have to wor - ry Well, some-
through.") ('bout ma - te - ri - al things) ('bout what - ev - er life brings).

It's too good to stop now, Fa - ther. I

BETTER

Words and Music by KIRK FRANKLIN,
VIDAL DAVIS and ANDRE HARRIS

Moderately fast

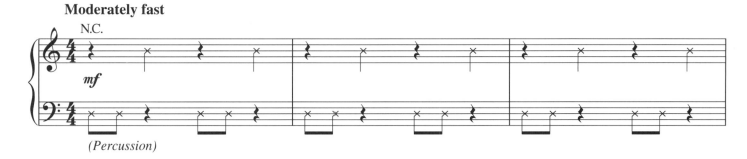

(Percussion)

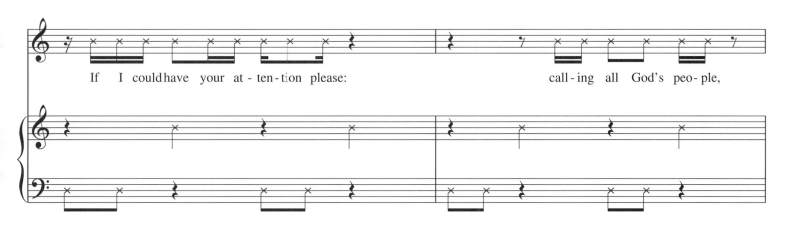

If I could have your at-ten-tion please: calling all God's peo-ple,

tell-ing 'em to get out of the dark-ness. Life is gon-na get

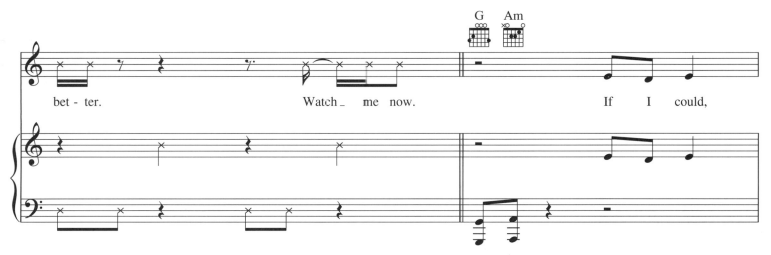

bet-ter. Watch me now. If I could,

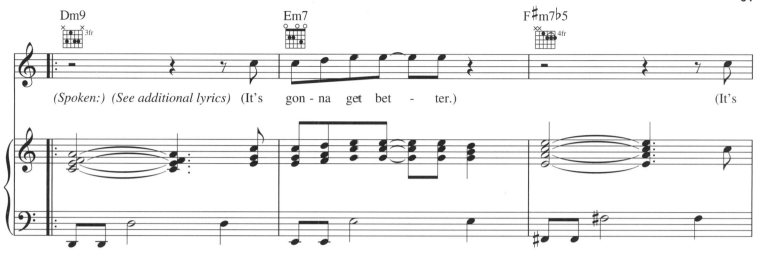

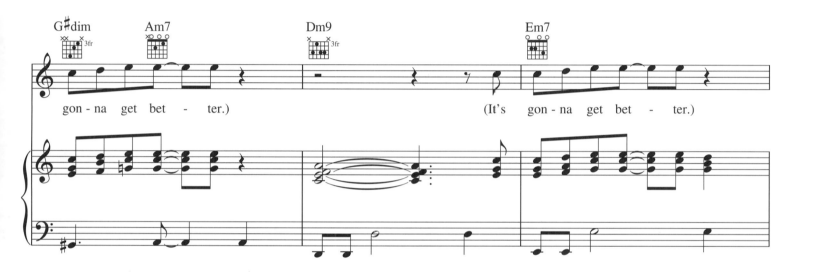

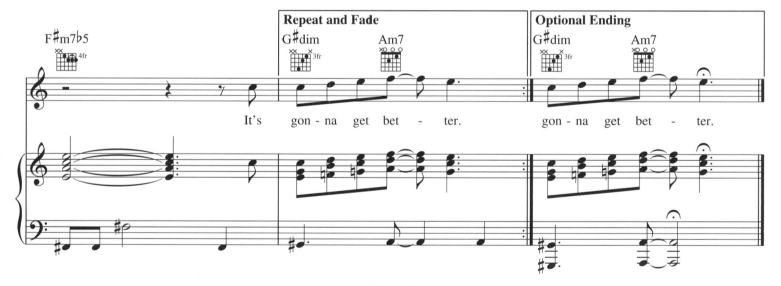

Additional Lyrics

So the next time you feel like giving up, remember . . .
The next time you feel like walking away, remember . . .
The next time you look at your bank account, remember . . .
The next time your child is in trouble, remember . . .

You're talking about your voice; just remember . . .
The next time you're crying in the midnight hour . . .
Look at somebody and tell them it's gonna, . . .

(ad lib. to fadeout)

AFTERWHILE

Words and Music by
KIRK FRANKLIN

Slowly

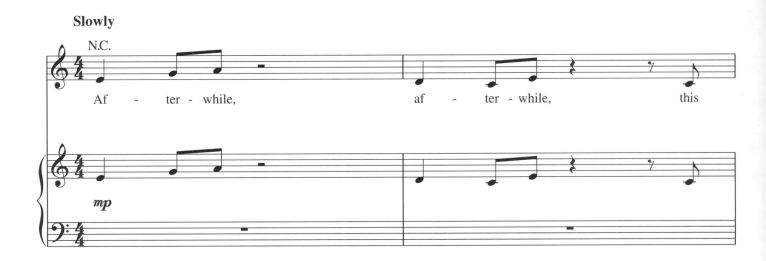

Af - ter - while, af - ter - while, this

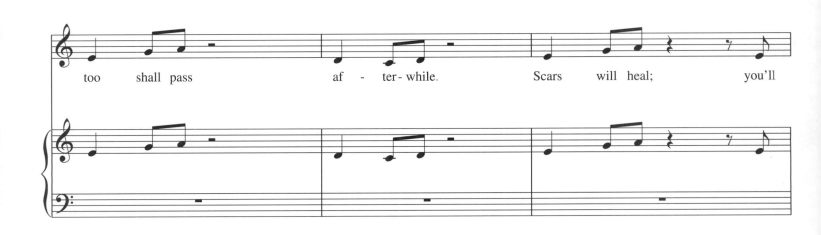

too shall pass af - ter - while. Scars will heal; you'll

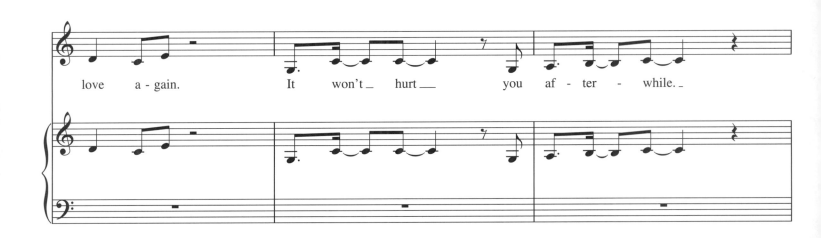

love a - gain. It won't _ hurt _ you af - ter - while. _

BROKENHEARTED

Words and Music by
KIRK FRANKLIN

*Recorded a half step higher.

WITHOUT YOU

Words and Music by
KIRK FRANKLIN

Moderately slow

I can take a plane high up in the sky and fly for a mil-lion miles, ____
I can see ____ the col-or of ____ spring, I can e-ven feel the weath-er change. ____ And
When I think ____ of where I've been, ____ what I've done and ____ what I own, ____

Play 3 times

write a mel-o-dy so sweet, make a tear turn in-to a smile. _
soon the leaves fall, _ the win-ter calls, noth-ing ev-er stays the same. _
how I think I know ev-'ry-thing, like I made it here _ on my own, ____

* Recorded a half step higher.

KEEP YOUR HEAD

Words and Music by
KIRK FRANKLIN

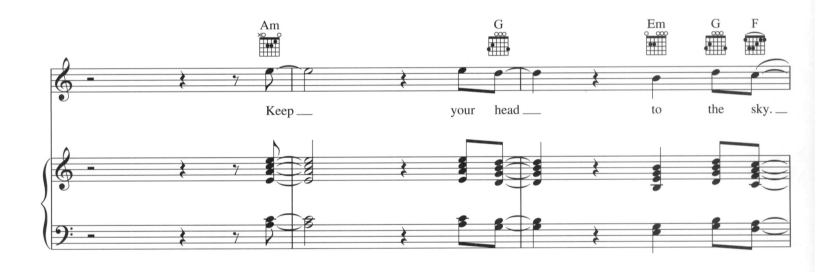

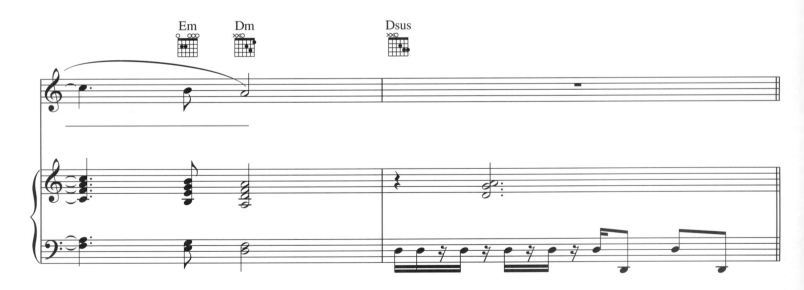

Rap: *(See additional lyrics)*

Keep _____ your head _____

Additional Lyrics

Clap your hands, y'all. All my
People, can you clap your hands? Let me hear you say.

(Yeah). If you know that things have gotta change, say
(Yeah), that nothing goes without a little rain, say
(Yeah), that no matter what they tell you, God is
Waiting and He's listening. Don't look back, 'cause it gets better.

(Yeah.) If you're blessed to have healthy kids, say
(Yeah). If you're blessed to have a place to live, say
(Yeah). Stop chasing after everything you see. May not have
Everything you want, but you've got everything you need.

WHY

Words and Music by
KIRK FRANKLIN

I pledge al - le-giance to the
___ We're kill - ing ba - bies and (I

(tell me what we gon' do).
love to see chil - dren play).

I used to know you but (you
I've got de - pres - sion. (There's a

Recorded a whole step lower.

FIRST LOVE

Words and Music by
KIRK FRANKLIN

(Spoken:) I just wanna talk to somebody right now who's been gone away for a long time:

You don't have to run no more; you can come back home.

I know they hurt __ you.
You did - n't make __ it;

They saw you stum - ble but did - n't help __ you, and now they left __ you.
you thought your love _____ would last for - ev - er. Ain't it fun - ny

* *Lead vocals recorded one octave lower.*

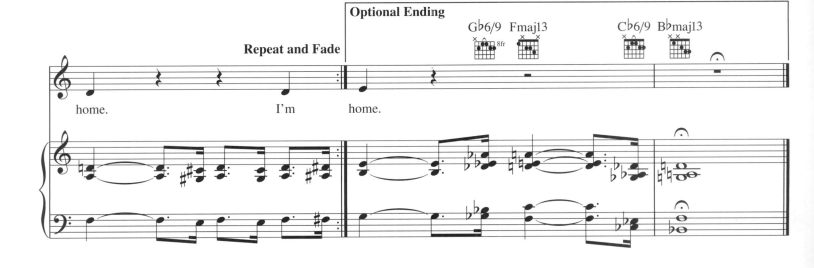

THE APPEAL

Words and Music by
KIRK FRANKLIN

Very slowly, expressively

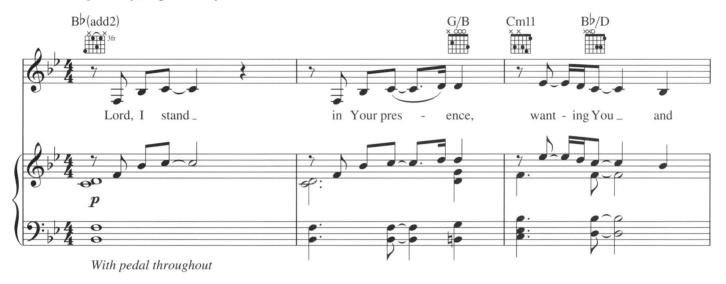

Lord, I stand _____ in Your pres - ence, want - ing You _____ and

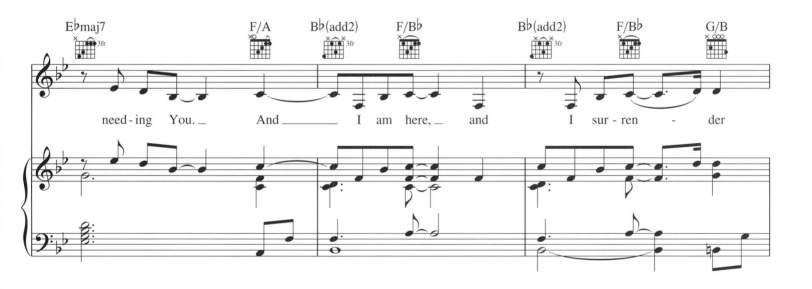

need - ing You. _____ And _____ I am here, _____ and I sur - ren - der

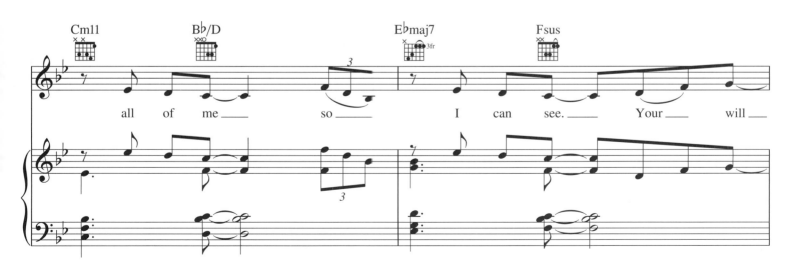

all of me _____ so _____ I can see. _____ Your _____ will _____

SUNSHINE

Words and Music by
KIRK FRANKLIN